VERANDA

Entertaining

VERANDA

Entertaining

Clinton Smith

HEARST
books

Introduction
—*page 7*

In the dining room of photographer Kate Cordsen's Victorian home in Connecticut, French doors are flung open to the breeze and a Moghul-inspired mural offsets a traditional table.

Veranda's previous books have focused on beautiful residences, stylized outdoor living, idyllic retreats, and gorgeous floral arrangements, the last of which is very much similar to entertaining. Entertaining and beautiful tablescapes have long been a cornerstone of the magazine's philosophy of gracious living. Just as there are "recipes" for great floral arrangements, there are ingredients for concocting a great party, however big or small. Food is an essential part of it, of course, but more than that, it's the environment, the mood, the spirit, the company, and the conversation that will last far longer than the memory of what anyone ate. The best dinner parties I've ever attended are the ones where I had the time of my life but can't recall a thing the host served.

The reason is that the hosts created a moment in time where no one thing superseded another and everything was in perfect harmony. A great party is often greater than the sum of its parts. It might look effortless, yet it's anything but, and renowned hosts should teach master classes on the art of entertaining. After nearly twenty years as a design and lifestyle journalist, I have attended hundreds of work-related dinners, black-tie galas, cocktail hours, soirees, and Sunday brunches; in fact, I eat out most nights of the week, except for weekends. So as much as I like to host a small dinner party, more often than not I am an observer of and participant in some of the best—and worst—entertaining experiences ever.

Here's what I know: People put too much emphasis on one part of an event. They focus exclusively on the centerpiece to the detriment of everything else on the table; they hire the best wedding photographer in the world, yet they get a store-bought cake; they try to make—on a first attempt—Julia Child's boeuf bourguignon for twelve and begin preparations right after lunch when guests are supposed to arrive at 7:00. All those things are a recipe for disaster. As a host, you're one part orchestra conductor, one part mind reader, and one part diplomat (yes, the talk of politics or religion at the table still needs to be handled delicately).

The purpose of this book is to share with you the entertaining ideals that *Veranda* holds dear, as well as things you can glean for your own Sunday suppers, afternoon teas, benefit galas, birthday parties, and intimate lunches. Let's raise a glass of rosé—here's to entertaining in style!

Clinton Smith
Veranda Editor in Chief

A bistro table and comfortable seating offer a warm welcome at Kathryn M. Ireland's farmhouse in Provence, France.

Alfresco

What is it about eating outdoors that makes one's troubles seemingly melt away? Maybe it's the sun-dappled light, a cooling cross breeze, or our primal connection to nature—or all of the above. Dining alfresco can be a transportive experience, recalling faraway places or memorable vacations from long ago. A perfect alfresco meal can be as casual as picnic tables lined up on a sandy perch with barefoot guests stretching the long day into a languorous summer night, or as elegant as a dining room table brought outside and topped off with a beautiful matelassé or Otomi-print cloth, recalling the South of France or a Oaxacan retreat. Ideally when dining alfresco, simpler is better: farm-fresh salads, bottles of rosé, and boughs of hydrangeas or sunflowers for centerpieces; a scattering of a dozen or so flickering tea lights will last the evening, or as long as the wine and conversation are flowing. Dining alfresco should be magical, and besides providing comfort for your guests, nothing should be superfluous. Let nature be your adornment and decoration.

right: Alliums clipped from the cutting garden make for a simple arrangement that's steeped in a sense of place. *below:* Refreshments can be crafted from what's on hand, like a summery cocktail made from fresh strawberries. *opposite:* With a few simple linens, afternoon aperitifs set up on the terrace need little more than geraniums and basil to feel special.

Simpler is better: bite size canapés bottles of rosé, *boughs of fresh flowers* for centerpieces.

clockwise from top left: A bounty of fresh produce, like homegrown tomatoes ripening on the vine, needs little in the way of embellishment. / A straight-forward pizza features thinly sliced zucchini and a dusting of cheese. / A repurposed jelly jar filled with fresh-cut flowers is a breezy addition to the spread. / Casserole dishes of pasta go from the stove directly to the table, along with a salad and a steaming pile of *moules marinière*. / Gazpacho and a simple salad. *opposite:* Guests serve themselves family-style on the shady lawn.

A trellised dining area by Mario Nievera and Markham Roberts is a magical oasis in a lush Palm Beach garden.

Ambience

There are a lot of things that can go wrong when you entertain—a *lot*—whether it's brunch, lunch, dinner, cocktails, or even breakfast in bed. I'll discuss the entire list throughout, but in the meantime, there is one important thing that you can control: ambience. When it's done correctly, nobody will notice (sorry!), but if you get it wrong, you'll be the talk of the neighborhood (and not in a good way—again, sorry!). Call it what you will—mood lighting, candlelight, dinner under the stars. And create it however you can—flickering votives, pendants on dimmers, moonlight, flameless pillars. Ambience is simple and straightforward, yet many people dismiss it, ignore it, or forget it. There are so many other unknown variables when you entertain—invitations lost in the mail, last-minute cancellations, mess-ups in the kitchen, soufflés that fall flat—so make ambience your first priority and check it off your list ahead of time.

The warm glow of candlelight casts a magical atmosphere in the Haussmann-era Paris apartment of ceramist Marie Daâge.

left: At her home in Gstaad, Switzerland, designer Michelle Nussbaumer introduces a riotous mix of rich blooms to set the mood. *opposite:* Designer Kelli Ford brings a global sensibility to her Dallas home.

It's probably the one thing you can do a month in advance! But note: If you only see your dining room or entertaining space in the daytime and are planning on entertaining at night, don't be surprised if the picture-perfect evening you envisioned doesn't live up to the dream. A friend of mine always found her dining room too dark, so she created a table runner out of small mirrors to reflect the flickering candlelight. The effect was stunning, and everyone looked their best.

from left: Mary McDonald decks the halls of her Beverly Hills house. / White anemones strike a note of quiet elegance.

from left: At dusk, Michelle Nussbaumer's Swiss chalet beckons. / Silver mugs of eggnog are welcome on chilly winter nights.

left: A selection of cheeses and white wine in a Palm Beach loggia make for an easy and satisfying cocktail hour. *below:* Bite-size nibbles are perfect party staples. This spread includes cured meats, olives, and *bulots,* or whelks, classic Provençal fare. *opposite:* Shawn Henderson lets guests help themselves in his laid-back upstate New York cottage.

Appetizers

Finger foods, canapés, hors d'oeuvres. Whatever you call them, they prove the adage that good things come in small packages. But a few words of advice: If you have waitstaff serving, don't choose anything that requires more than one hand to eat. Your guests will have to come up with awkward, acrobatic moves to juggle their wineglass and a plate while trying to hold a beef slider with both hands—it's neither a pretty nor a gracious scene. And please don't pass nibbles that require guests to think about where to stash a dirty toothpick, shrimp carcass, or empty skewer afterward; provide them with an easy solution for disposal, even if it's just an extra napkin. Finally, make sure you offer enough food to balance out the alcohol consumed during cocktail hour. No one enjoys a tipsy dinner companion.

clockwise from top left: Mild cheeses on blue-and-white porcelain. / A cake platter is a unique way to present viands. / Olives, capers, and toasted bread are perfect accompaniments. / Small bites should be offered with an assortment of wine and spirits. / Seeded breadsticks are flavorful and fuss-free. *opposite:* Blini and caviar is an elegant, classic pairing.

A well-designed kitchen, such as this New York space by Peter Dunham, can make entertaining feel effortless.

Basics

What do you need to entertain? Whether it's a successful party for a dozen or a casual dinner for a few friends on a Tuesday night, preparedness is key. If you're always scrambling to put something together, you'll never do it right. Being a great entertainer and host is about having a well-stocked pantry and bar at the ready. (Don't forget the mixers!) Being able to call upon a cadre of recipes that you can prepare in a flash will make everything much easier and less daunting. If you're not a cook, a roast chicken from the local market can be a lifesaver. One of the best dinner parties I ever attended was when the host served thin flatbread pizzas with Gruyère and ham and a lightly dressed arugula salad along with a few bottles of Chianti. Luckily, she confided the pizza's provenance—her grocer's freezer. One other rule of entertaining: Don't be afraid to ask for help. Whether it's calling upon the prepared-foods section at the market or hiring someone to man the bar and serve drinks (and assist with cleanup), having extra hands to help out can go a long way in making for a stress-free evening.

right: A holiday table by Keith Robinson combines a few simple ingredients—boxwood, amaryllis, and rosemary sprigs—that elegantly elevates his Georgia barn. *below:* Serving pieces can be both stylish and utilitarian. *opposite:* With an armada of pots overhead and a meal ready to be served family-style, designer Windsor Smith's kitchen marries form with function.

Having a well-stocked kitchen and a few *go-to recipes* make for ease of entertaining.

left: A mousse-filled pastry takes the shape of a swan. *below:* A medley of pattern and color draws the eye to the table in Charlotte Moss's East Hampton house. *opposite:* Afternoon tea in Susan Gutfreund's New York apartment offers a glamorous moment of repose.

Beauty

This may seem like a rather silly entry since, after all, we all want to be surrounded by beauty (or at least one would hope). But the difference between something that's simply nice and lovely and something that's truly beautiful, whether a tablescape, invitation, or food presentation, is the extra care and thought that goes into each and every decision. Even with a hectic schedule, it's not impossible to make something truly beautiful. Remove the stress by just inviting over another couple instead of orchestrating a get-together for twelve. That way, you can go the extra mile in creating something truly distinctive for people you care about instead of spreading your resources too thin. Having lunch with a friend? Create an arrangement made with her favorite flowers. It's the little gestures that make moments of lasting beauty.

Beauty is about honoring your guests by creating an environment filled with magical touches.

For the festive season, Stephen Sills's library features organic holiday decor that complements the room's natural beauty. An intimate dining table is set for dessert.

Bliss

Bliss is one of those things that is difficult to delineate, yet it is a building block for any sort of intimate sit-down meal or grand convocation. People want to feel special, plain and simple. If you can't ensure a pleasant, pleasurable sitting for each person in attendance, don't bother. Of course, there are always unforeseen surprises, even mishaps in the kitchen, but the best guest will understand and overlook them (and they'll be the ones who'll get invited back first)! Ironing out an agenda ahead of time and trying to anticipate what might go wrong will help you ward off any problems that may arise. Your best bet: Pretend that you are a guest, not the host, and do a simple walk-through of the evening, beginning to end, from their perspective. That process begins well before they get a drink in hand. What is the experience when your guests park their car? Is the sidewalk well lit? Who is answering the door? Where do you store the coats, and are there enough hangers? If you're left fumbling with those details before the party has even started, your guests are surely not going to feel bliss, but perhaps they'll feel blah.

Along Florida's Gulf Coast, designer Susan Ferrier created a casually elegant outdoor living space that maximizes its oceanfront views, especially at sunset when dinner is served.

left: Designer John Saladino creates a magical dining oasis underneath a canopy of ancient olive trees.
below: Sunflowers surrounding Kathryn M. Ireland's Provence property are used in centerpiece arrangements. *opposite:* Expansive water views are the focal point of porch dinners at Kate Cordsen's Connecticut haven.

Creating a *blissful experience* for guests begins the moment the invitation is sent.

An elegant evening at Windsor Smith's Los Angeles home includes twinkling lanterns on the table, the warmth of a roaring fire, and flickering tapers on wall brackets, which heighten the room's drama.

Candlelight

Ah, candlelight. It would not be impossible, or even a stretch, to write an entire tome on the importance of candlelight, yet I'm relegated here to a few passages to extol its virtues. Everyone looks better in candlelight, so that should be the first and foremost reason to light a few wicks. In fact, it's reason enough. What is remarkable is how one teeny, tiny flicker of a flame can enhance the mood of a space so dramatically. It can single-handedly change a room's energy. Better yet, the warmth, the glow, and the romance are compounded with each and every candle you light. Maybe it's a single tall taper ensconced in a hurricane lantern, or two silver candelabras on each end of a table. Maybe an amalgamation of disparate styles—brass! glass! crystal!—commingle to create a unified look. Whichever route you take, don't underestimate the power of a warm glow—and remember to keep the overhead lights turned off or dimmed very low. Your guests will thank you.

Dan Belman and Randy Korando's Georgia barn features a candlelit chandelier wrapped in greenery, faux-antler candleholders, and a tree laden with strings and strings of sparkling lights.

from left: Tea lights and hurricane lanterns illuminate the terrace of Quinn Pofahl and Jaime Jiménez's historic Hamptons home, where they often entertain in the summer. / Candles cast light on a portrait and highlight holiday greenery in Mary McDonald's California abode.

from left: Veere Grenney and David Oliver's holiday tablescape features tapers at varying heights for added interest, with flowers by Shane Connolly. / Exquisite candelabras are the perfect juxtaposition against rough-hewn paneling in Michelle Nussbaumer's Swiss chalet.

At their farm near Atlanta, Dan Belman and Randy Korando create a theatrical, equestrian-inspired holiday setting in their horse barn.

The grand dining room of Ann Getty's San Francisco home hosts everything from Sunday dinners to festive holiday soirees.

Centerpieces

One of the most important focal points of any gathering at a table, the centerpiece is also often one of the most poorly considered. I have attended countless large-scale events over the years, including black-tie galas, charity luncheons, and weddings, and I would say that a huge percentage have had unfortunate centerpieces. Even in residential settings, where they may be less intrusive, the same simple rules apply: Don't obstruct the view of other guests, the keynote speaker, or the guest of honor; don't employ scented flowers that might overpower the taste of the food; and don't make the centerpiece the only star of the show. A memorable event isn't measured by the height, scale, and profusion of flowers in a centerpiece—it's the sum of those things, plus the food, the guests, and, most importantly, the conversation and the purpose of the occasion.

from left: Hutton Wilkinson creates a unique composition of orange ranunculus and berries still on their branches. / Richard Keith Langham uses fiery-red carnations to dramatic effect.

from left: Gold accent pieces add luster to Ann Getty's dining table. / Paperwhites mimic the pared-down palette in a dining space by Mary McDonald.

China

First and foremost, setting the table should be fun! Whether it's formal or fancy-free, rustic or regal, don't be afraid to mix and match patterns. And remember: A little whimsy is always welcome, even for the swankiest soirees.

Cocktails

Everyone has a favorite drink. If your event is intimate, ask your guests in advance if anyone has a preferred libation. A full bar is always a thoughtful consideration, but for larger events a signature cocktail, plus wine, is acceptable. Be careful not to create something too sugary, too complicated, or downright unpalatable. If in doubt, get a taste tester to give you a second opinion. I once attended a holiday party where the specialty cocktail was a sickly concoction. The rim of the glass was copiously covered in crushed peppermint. It was too sweet to drink, and every time you took a sip, you had a mouthful of crunchy candy to chew and eat. The most popular signature cocktails seem to be those with a few ingredients plus vodka (Moscow Mule, anyone?), gin (who doesn't love a Gin Rickey?), or maybe rum (yum, mojitos!). Margaritas are always popular too, but whichever drink you choose to serve, remember to keep the sugary mixes at a minimum and the components fresh and pure.

Collections

Not everyone is lucky enough to inherit his or her great-grandmother's china, not to mention the accompanying crystal, heirloom linens, and coveted family silver. However, there are many ways to fast-track a collection while still purchasing quality. You can buy new, of course, and there are some wildly spectacular china and cut-crystal patterns that will be future inheritances. When shopping, the key is to have an open mind, a keen eye, and a willingness to look at the unexpected. Consider surveying online repositories that sell antique and vintage replacement flatware and china. Oftentimes, these sites can be a gold mine for beautiful, classic pieces that have been discontinued by a manufacturer, yet remain as timeless as ever. Old Paris porcelain

right: With the addition of greenery and flowers, a display of blue-and-white china can change with the season. *opposite:* Event designer Keith Robinson's collection of porcelain—he owns more than 800 vintage pieces—is an element of his dining room decor.

can be had for a steal in *brocantes,* although you may have to cobble it together a few pieces at a time (but that's part of the fun). Auction houses conduct "house" sales that feature interior objets from many different collections, and estate sales are worth checking out for antique French Champagne coupes, unusual serving pieces (oyster forks, anyone?), and unique handmade pottery. Note that a collection doesn't have to match. Instead of focusing on one particular pattern for a place setting, think about a particular genre instead: English transferware, for instance, or Portuguese pottery, French terre mêlée or Italian Murano-glass tumblers. Part of the fun of a collection is that you can mix and match to create a one-of-a-kind tablescape that represents your personality as much as the rest of your decor.

At Bunny Williams's Connecticut home, even a mismatched grouping of objects can have enormous appeal when displayed en masse and organized by shape and hue.

Collections shouldn't be about finery and provenance. Whether it's a grouping of disparate flea-market finds or inherited heirloom silver, you should live with the things you love *everyday,* not just on special occasions.

A varied selection of stemware—like the bohemian glasses and silver goblets Robert Couturier set out buffet-style in Connecticut—can create a vivid display.

Robert Couturier sets up post-lunch coffee in the cozy salon of his Connecticut house.

Comfort

Even in the most elegant environment, comfort is defined by the simplest pleasures: a warm cup of tea, a plush place to sit, and the exchange of conversation among friends.

In her Paris apartment, Marie Daâge uses compotes for centerpieces and arranges sweets on mismatched footed plates.

Desserts

I firmly believe that the cheese course is overrated. A couple of nice blocks of cheese along with some dates, almonds, walnuts, grapes, and honey may be delicious after dinner, but I often feel so satiated already that I secretly wish I could take the platter home for tomorrow afternoon's snack! (I would never dare.) In restaurants, desserts often seem overly complicated and sophisticated while being insufficiently tasty to merit the calories. That's why I am a strong advocate for fruit gelati, ice creams, and sorbets—classic chocolate and vanilla and maybe pistachio and mint chocolate for good measure. It never fails that one scoop always turns into two! A few biscotti or pieces of dark chocolate, perhaps served with a teeny glass of port, allow guests to choose how indulgent they want to be. All of these offerings are simple gestures, which is what I think people desire when gathering with friends.

right: The holidays call for indulging, and this mouthwatering spread in Alabama was curated by Tammy Connor. *below:* Mini panettones are encircled with dried oranges and garnished with ribbon-wrapped cinnamon sticks. *opposite:* A buffet by Elizabeth Locke in South Carolina is a discreet way to let guests choose their own portions.

Never underestimate the *power and joy* of a sinfully decadent dessert.

from left: A Bundt cake on an etched pedestal needs little more than a dusting of coconut flakes to carry a sense of occasion. / Poached pears and mini panna cottas are light and simple.

from left: Individual croquembouches, paired with Venetian glassware and a Persian vase, are a dramatic finale. / Coffee *pots de crème* are delightful served in demitasse cups.

Details

Some say "It's all in the details," while others dismiss such minutiae with a wave of the hand: "Details, details, details." But as any successful host knows, the devil is in the details, and the little things do matter. Whether it's making sure the linens are pressed and the silver polished for a formal evening, or the Chinet and fried chicken are beautifully arranged in the picnic hamper, it is the sum of the many individual elements that create a warm and welcoming environment, and no detail is small enough to overlook. That's not to say that a conscious concern for the particulars should overwhelm or become onerous when planning your beautiful event. A little planning and foresight will make your evening (or afternoon outing) more carefree for you, and thus make your guests feel more welcomed and relaxed. Make lists, and shop and order well ahead of time; double-check on deliveries; and set out everything the night before. The element of surprise is fantastic for your guests, but as the host with the most, you don't want to be the one surprised.

An embroidered tablecloth echoes patterns in Marie Daâge's china, which she purposely mismatches for another layer of visual interest.

Marie

left: Marie Daâge's dining room walls are painted verdigris, an 18th-century shade that goes with everything. *below:* Tammy Connor hangs diminutive stockings so they appear to dangle from branches painted on the wallpaper. *opposite:* In Gstaad, Michelle Nussbaumer piles pattern on pattern on pattern to create a riotous delight for the eyes.

The element of surprise is great for guests, but not for the host. Keeping an eye on the *details* makes all the difference.

An elegant table in Kate Cordsen's Connecticut home is a simple composition of textures and materials—crystal, silver, linen—which play off one another and refract gorgeous natural light.

Essentials

Few things in life are essential, but many things are desirable! And when entertaining, we often become so distracted by the desire to make an impression and ensure that everything is perfect that we actually lose sight of what is most essential: the comfort of your guests. Good manners prevent your guests from asking who else is invited, but I say go ahead and tell them. Even better, plan your seating chart well ahead of time and let everyone know a tidbit or two about his or her dinner mates. Nothing is more boring or uncomfortable, especially in an intimate environment, than when the host asks everyone upon sitting down to introduce themselves to the others and say something about him- or herself. Surprisingly enough, in this age of tireless self-promotion and social media, many of the most interesting people remain modest. Know your company and be sensitive to everyone's likes and dislikes. That's essential!

Selina van der Geest's well-stocked kitchen
includes plenty of options for serving and an
open-plan layout that simplifies prep work.
The island is also a central gathering spot for
family and friends.

right: With a gleaming butler's pantry, Amanda Nisbet created a convenient—and visually compelling—staging ground for a client in New York. *opposite:* In a Nashville kitchen by Bobby McAlpine, tableware and utensils are always within arm's reach. *below:* A handwritten menu card is a charming grace note for the table.

Entertaining essentials should include everything from good manners to good company.

In his Beverly Hills garden, Hutton Wilkinson creates a plein-air fantasia.

F

Fantasy

One person's fantasy is another person's routine. In an increasingly connected and globalized world, the foreign and unknown are still, surprisingly, unknown. Sometimes something forgotten can suddenly become imbued with a sense of exoticism simply through its deployment at the table. Think of ways to use the usual and overlooked in unusual spots, or go in the opposite direction and create an otherworldy space for your guests. Tell everyone in advance a word or theme—think bold colors or faraway locales or a point of time in history—that will inform the evening and let guests be part of the decor. Select unique foods and styles of presentation apart from the ordinary and everyday.

Flatware

Good taste is often exhibited on the table before the first bite of food is sampled, and beautiful and unique flatware is a way to convey a sense of personal style and your flair for entertaining.

Flowers

You've probably been to a dinner where the flowers on the table have been so big that you can't see above them, much less around them, so you're relegated to talking to the dinner companions on your immediate right and left all evening long (for better or worse). Wading through a floral arrangement to talk to someone across the table seems like an obvious entertaining offense, yet it still happens frequently. The other faux pas: scented flowers with so much perfume, they overpower the taste of the food and wine. A low centerpiece overflowing with majestic fruits and vegetables is of little value if it's as big as the table itself and leaves little room for serving food, putting down a wineglass, or even excusing oneself from the table. I don't like decorating rules, even less so when they apply to entertaining, but flowers should be incorporated into a tabletop scheme wisely, rather than just on their good looks alone.

Under a bower of Lady Banks roses, Keith Robinson's garden provides an eye-popping backdrop for lunch.

right: Matching low posies in a Palm Beach garden pavilion by Markham Roberts bring romance to the table but still allow for guests to make eye contact. *below:* Foliage and kumquats play against the rich hue of pink ranunculus. *opposite:* A mix of dahlias and berries feels deliciously down-to-earth in a wicker centerpiece at Colette van den Thillart's Canadian wilderness retreat.

After food, *flowers* are one of the most recalled elements of an event. Their importance can't be underestimated.

left: In Gstaad, Michelle Nussbaumer blends different blooms in the same hue and deploys unexpected receptacles like pitchers. *below:* To play off the patterns in vintage porcelain, Keith Robinson pairs flowers and china. *opposite:* A profusion of a single kind of bloom, like this beautiful centerpiece by Robinson made entirely from hydrangeas, can have a dramatic impact.

Whether mininal or over-the-top, flowers add a *dramatic* touch to any gathering.

from left: In a Montecito, California, house by Christina Rottman, peonies and tulips pick up tones in the place settings. / Apples and magnolia leaves can feel as festive as a julep cup filled with ranunculus.

from left: Charlotte Moss channels sunny tones with tree peonies and lilies in a porcelain cachepot. / Dusty-pink variegated peonies match the pretty pastel shades of ranunculus and hydrangeas.

left: Bibelots galore give an outdoor setting at Hutton Wilkinson's Beverly Hills estate the feel of a fancy-dress ball. *below:* Peacock feathers and citrus are sumptuous holiday elements in Mary McDonald's California abode. *opposite:* Gleaming wallpaper, patent-leather cushions, and a sparkling Swedish chandelier up the ante in a Dallas dining room by Julie Hayes.

Formality

The word *formality* is often met with the same disregard as receiving an invitation to one's class reunion. In the restaurant world, fine dining is no longer de rigueur. White-tablecloth manners, chef's special preparations, and the general sense of decorum that have long been staples of fine dining have been replaced with novelty drinks, decibel-busting dining spaces, and farm-to-table fetishes. That former elegance has long since gone the way of airline travel: There's little decorum left. But you can remedy that! The equivalent of flying privately is to entertain at home. You still don't need to pull out a white tablecloth, but you should consider how to best honor your guests. Maybe prepare a handwritten menu or leave them with a small parting gift. Don't equate formality with finger bowls or ten-course tasting menus; rather, it's a respect for the world you're creating and people you're hosting.

Etched glasses in varying heights and shapes are especially refined in architect James Carter's traditionally inflected Georgian-style house in Birmingham, Alabama.

Glassware

If you entertain, you need a lot of glassware. A lot. Whether it's by unwieldy guests or a mangling dishwasher, so much of it gets broken, the fine stuff and the everyday. Best to brace yourself for the inevitable by buying extra and accepting reality—it really helps. The demands for imbibing are more than you may think: juice glasses, water glasses, wineglasses, highballs, tumblers, flutes, and coupes—the list goes on and on. Stocking up? Start with the necessities first, then add supporting pieces as you see fit. (Do you really need to buy a dozen brandy snifters?) My advice: Test out a glass before buying dozens of each. I love weighty, wrist-wrenching glassware, while a friend prefers pieces that are as thin as ice. Will it load in the dishwasher easily or need to be hand-washed? Clear crystal and glass is always a sure bet. Colored glasses are pretty for holding water and perhaps white wine, but remember that colored liquids in colored glasses aren't always easy on the eyes or easy to swallow—pun intended.

clockwise from top left: Colored glasses add dimension to a bright table. / Swirling ribbed glasses are subtly sophisticated. / Graphic shapes riff on vibrant stripes. / Flutes double as streamlined bud vases. / A classic shape adapts well to water or cocktails. *opposite:* A Murano goblet catches brandy hues.

Platinum-rimmed glasses add sparkle to a graceful monochromatic table in Alessandra Branca's New York pied-à-terre.

Sip and savor the good life with gorgeous *glassware*, from sinuous Champagne flutes to stout ceramic tumblers. Varying heights of drinking vessels on a table offer endless appeal—we'll drink to that!

Richard Keith Langham has made a tradition of decorating his Manhattan showroom for the holidays with bold, sweeping gestures, such as this towering tree, which grazes the 22-foot-tall ceilings.

Holidays

Oh, the holidays! Christmas, New Year's, the Fourth of July, Valentine's Day, National Margarita Day... the list is endless. Whichever it is, whatever the month, there's always a cause for celebration. As frivolous as some of them may seem, isn't each holiday reason enough to have a party? People are often afraid to entertain because so many occasions for getting people together rest upon big events, such as weddings, birthdays, graduations, and other milestone moments. The idea of hosting the perfect event to memorialize the occasion becomes paralyzing. So don't do it! And yes, many of the holidays are big events too, but they shouldn't incite the same anticipation or anxiety as hosting a wedding or 21st-birthday party. Maybe you should just have a dinner party because it's Wednesday night and the workweek is half over. But if you have to have a reason, I can assure you that there's a National Something Day tomorrow and every remaining day this year.

right: Tammy Connor's Christmas table is elegantly pared down, with paperwhites, bowls of oranges, and graceful wooden stags. *below:* A tiered candy dish is decorative as well as delicious. *opposite:* In her Long Island barn, Aerin Lauder mingles Austrian antiques with pine boughs and pops of pattern.

From Christmas to National Cat Day, there's a *holiday*—and a reason to celebrate— every day of the year.

Citrus, ribbon-wrapped cinnamon sticks, and gracefully weathered architectural elements and antiques add up to an elegant, unstudied holiday setting in Connecticut.

clockwise from top left: Hand-painted wrapping paper is an artful departure from the expected. / Green stockings make a statement on a white hearth. / Traditional Christmas sparkle is always stylish. / Decorating the entryway is a festive way to say "Welcome!" / A pine-and-eucalyptus wreath is beautiful and fragrant. *opposite:* Ornaments await trimming in a New York apartment by Bill Brockschmidt and Courtney Coleman.

Pomegranate juice and arils turn flutes of Champagne into jewel-toned cocktails worthy of a celebration; paperwhites and a laurel-leaf topiary are a subtle nod to the season in a space by Tammy Connor.

When he entertains in Connecticut, Robert Couturier doesn't hesitate to gild the lily, serving such things as deviled quail eggs with foie gras, cherry-tomato caprese, and goat-cheese canapés.

Indulgences

I love an indulgence, and I know you do too. We often restrict our diets to what's healthy or quick and easy. Kale salads, quinoa everything, and juice cleanses seem to be the order of the day. But think about the oohs and aahs that accompany potato chips with a dollop of caviar and crème fraîche or the fleeting delight and delicacy of fried squash blossoms. It's important to note that there's a difference between indulgence and extravagance, and everyday indulgences are the best—and they don't have to be costly. Think of the titillation that comes from one bite of fresh melon wrapped in prosciutto, or the ephemeral feeling of a tomato sandwich so good that, like a time stamp, you know it's the middle of summer and the living is easy. The same goes for your tabletop. To make yourself and everyone else feel just a little bit indulgent, set the table with your simplest dishes and everyday flatware, then amp everything up with an over-the-top (but not too distracting) centerpiece or a bountiful platter of fresh, exotic fruits.

Intimacy

There's something about creating an intimate environment that makes for lasting bonds, both with old friends and new acquaintances. Intimacy comes when the setting encourages guests to move beyond small talk and chitchat and into topics that ignite passion points and activate communal thought. Perhaps it's a dinner in a dimly lit room, or a gossipy tête-à-tête among friends. The sharing of new ideas, inspirations, challenges faced, and hardships won builds enduring relationships. To be able to foster such an environment is a subtle gift, one learned through experience and study. Read the memoirs of some of society's most fabled hostesses—Lee Radziwill, Nan Kempner, and Florence Pritchett Smith, to name a few—there is a lot to learn there, and like good manners, good tricks to entertaining never go out of style.

In Alessandra Branca's Manhattan pied-à-terre, where space is at a premium, an English drop-leaf table is pulled up to a banquette in the study, and what seems like a limitation suddenly becomes a boon—cozy, romantic, and sumptuous.

from left: In a Palm Beach breakfast room by Markham Roberts, exotic art and charming prints sweep diners worlds away. / The New York City terrace of Michael S. Smith teems with blooms and foliage and affords stunning city views.

from left: China cabinets ensconce Laurann Claridge's Houston kitchen in cupfuls of charm. / A Virginia terrace by Suzanne Kasler is an ideal spot to while away an afternoon (or two).

An outdoor dining space by designer Christina Rottman epitomizes gracious entertaining with its casual elegance.

J

Joie de Vivre

The French have it in spades: that zest for pursuing the good life while enjoying life's simpler pleasures. How do you encourage an appreciation for the joy of living among your guests while navigating and managing all the details of your evening? Perhaps taking a page from the French playbook, the most important quality you can bring to entertaining is a sense of ease. If you are harried, hurried, worried, or uncomfortable, your guests will pick up on it in a heartbeat, and there goes the intimacy of the evening. The key to hospitality is to make everyone feel welcome through your effortless grace. The perfect dinner party always includes friends old and new as well as colleagues from diverse fields of interest and expertise. Treat intimates

right: Surrounded by vivid patterns, even a straightforward bowl of lemons is a thing of beauty. *opposite:* On Lipari, in the Aeolian Islands, Elda and Nicola Fabrizio revel in the Mediterranean lifestyle, growing their own vegetables, pressing their own olive oil, and eating alfresco all summer long.

and recent acquaintances with the same level of regard and interest. Don't suppose everyone can just take care of himself or herself—check back in at some point during cocktails and during dinner conversation. High on my list of don'ts: Don't make guests switch seating assignments for dessert. Intimacy and good conversation can't be forced, nor should they be disrupted by this circus trick if two of your guests are getting on like a house on fire.

With hand-painted wallpaper, matching curtains, and a forest's worth of boughs and greenery, Charlotte Moss transforms her Manhattan brownstone's dining room into a chic bower.

clockwise from top left: Festive greenery elevates an Aspen mudroom. / Holidays are extra special with a towering tree. / Paperwhites and amaryllis upgrade a gift-wrapping station. / A pond boat adds whimsy to an entertaining pavilion. / Start the evening with a cheese course. *opposite:* Lunch in the courtyard of Ralph Lauren's Paris restaurant is a deliciously drawn-out affair.

In a tablesetting for a New York client, Hutton Wilkinson displays his fearless embrace of color, pattern, and light.

K

Kaleidoscope

Kaleidoscope might sound like a curious entry, but color and pattern—and a certain type of devil-may-care verve—are just a few things missing from today's tablescapes. I'm a big advocate for simplicity, restraint, and understated elegance, but the sea of white plates, white tablecloths, and clear glassware that has taken over America's dining rooms could use a heaping dose of personality. True, people are scared of bold palettes, and yes, it's easier to commit to a red throw pillow than a red sofa. It's the same for china and linens; they can be expensive, so people are less willing to take chances with a palette or pattern they might regret in ten years. If you must buy neutral dinnerware, definitely go for bold with a large, colorful charger for serving or a contrasting dinner napkin packed with personality. And blanket your table in all sorts of flowers in various colors. Their ephemeral quality makes them more memorable to the mind's eye.

Hutton Wilkinson conjures a sophisticated refuge with a riot of disparate materials, from jade-green velvet to a leopard-print carpet to antique chairs he painted with a felt-tip pen.

A bright, florid monogram takes center stage in a wildly inventive tablesetting by Michelle Nussbaumer.

Linens

It's rare these days for people to have a classic trousseau. From Victorian times through to the 1950s, a classic trousseau included clothing, housewares, collectibles like china handed down through generations, and fine linens. These days, the rules are broken and a few good sets will take you from family dinners to feasts and fetes. Monograms—a longtime staple of any beautiful table—are now available in brilliant color combinations and modern designs, which have taken a classic into the 21st century. What's more, if you'd rather not have an instant set of hand-stitched linens, beautiful old French tea towels often feature subtle, hand-embroidered initials, as well as a softness that only comes with age.

right: Periwinkle napkins coordinate with a chocolate-brown fabric and flowers by Keith Robinson. *below:* A classic embroidered tablecloth creates a timeless backdrop in Paris. *opposite:* A nubby neutral linen has a plainspoken beauty on Elizabeth Locke's South Carolina porch.

Pretty *linens* can be demure and a quiet complement to the decor, or bold and the life of the party.

Whether colorful or quiet, hand-stitched or heirloom, *Linens* have to be just one thing: hardworking. (And good-looking, but that's a given.) So take them out of the drawer and use them—every single day!

from left: A subtle herringbone pattern makes a good foil for a monogrammed napkin in an updated, happy shade. / A mélange of verdant hues creates a symphony of color.

from left: Vintage linens bring a soupçon of charm to Susan Gutfreund's opulent living room. / A mix of textures and patterns is a lively way of keeping a table from feeling too static.

A casual embroidered tablecloth is a
breezy counterpoint to the glimmering
formality of a Palm Beach dining room.

In his Istanbul pied-à-terre, Antony Todd sets out an array of mezes, traditional Turkish appetizers, for guests to graze on with cocktails.

Menu

Simplicity is elegance, and your menu planning should reflect that. If devising the perfect meal proves to be an ongoing challenge, reconsider your options. I'm not advocating taking a poorly conceived shortcut with recipes and ingredients, but rather following the lead of the best hosts who know how to prioritize where it matters without sacrificing taste, quality, or that "wow" factor. For a spring brunch, the first course consists of something chilled, such as a cooling gazpacho that can be prepared in advance, yet will taste as fresh as if it were made that morning. In the winter, serve your guests a one-pot meal, perhaps an easy stew that you've let simmer all day. Paired with a crusty French baguette, a simple salad, and a robust bottle of red wine from the cellar, dinner is complete! If all else fails, call a caterer. A good menu always reflects the season and highlights what is fresh and local; it also celebrates the occasion without being contrived or precious. And a gracious host always asks guests to let him or her know of food allergies or dietary restrictions well in advance of the event.

clockwise from top left: An indulgent risotto is a showcase for white truffles. / Smoked salmon and traditional accompaniments are brunch staples. / Grape leaves and berries on the branch are a clever garnish for cheese. / Steamed lobster is served simply adorned. / Keep olives and cheese on hand for an impromptu cocktail hour. *opposite:* A pie festooned with a pastry heart adds a sweet note to the dinner table of Aerin Lauder in Aspen.

A buffet-style approach for the holidays eases pressure on the host and lets guests serve themselves at their own pace.

Keith Robinson matches rough spun–linen napkins with hand-tied rings crafted from rosemary.

Napkin Rings

It has been said many times, and it's still true: Napkin rings are jewelry for the table. Dressing the table is not unlike dressing oneself—it's wearing a uniform of classic white shirt and black trousers and then accenting that same outfit, day after day, with different earrings or a statement necklace. Countless combinations enliven the outfit, giving it new personality and life. And just as easily, a quick change can take you from day into evening. The same holds true at the table. Even if you eat with the exact same dinnerware, flatware, and linens every day (and I doubt most of us are using a different set of china for breakfast every morning), napkin rings allow you to transform the table to reflect your mood, from casual or classic to formal or flirty. The best part is that because even the finest ones aren't expensive, you can accessorize your table to your heart's content.

Silver-plated rings mingle with sunny stripes, blue-and-white porcelain, and gold accents in the courtyard of Ralph Lauren's Paris eatery.

Glimmering mirrors and crystal, gleaming porcelain, and acres of gilt combine with muted jewel tones to create a truly sumptuous dining room in Ann Getty's San Francisco home.

Opulence

Many of us make the assumption that opulence requires wealth—that it necessarily connotes a display of affluence. What the most successful hosts know, however, is that opulence at the dinner table does not require great financial resources, ostentatious displays of silver and china, or hordes of servers attending to everyone's needs. True opulence can be found through an abundant presentation of sumptuous foods. That doesn't mean a parade of the most expensive cuts of meat, exotically sourced foods, or the presentation of a veritable banquet. The perfectly opulent party is one where everything is perfectly prepared and presented, regardless of its provenance. The most splendid dinner might be composed of nothing more than delicious cheeses, olives, baguettes, charcuterie, and wine: The secret is making sure that everything is delicious and plentiful. Even the most humble foods, say, a platter of crudités, appear lavish in great abundance.

An intimate lunch in Susan Gutfreund's "winter garden" envelops guests in hand-carved trellises, painted floral panels, and taffeta curtains, all conceived by the late decorator Henri Samuel.

For lunch on his terrace, Michael S. Smith mixes and matches with ease. Here, he pairs custom Spanish plates and napkins, vintage flatware, and chartreuse and burgundy sedum.

Place Settings

Mastering the art of the perfect place setting is about celebrating its imperfections. If every single thing is just so, there's a real chance it can appear forced or stiff. Creating a tablescape that's at ease is not the same as being sloppy or careless. Even for the most formal occasions, something that's not "just so" adds an element of intrigue and is often a conversation starter. Mixing and matching china is an obvious start—it is surprising yet retains its elegance—but whimsical place cards, napkins folded in interesting ways, and colored glassware can also turn a table decorated in good taste into one that's easy on the eyes.

right: Creamy graphic china is extra pretty next to wooden accents.
below: Braided water-hyacinth placemats and splatterware plates add dimension and texture. *opposite:* Crimson blossoms inspire a floral tablecloth and gingham napkins.

The secret to putting together a perfect *place setting* is to keep it from being *too* perfect.

from left: A paper sculpture and traditional Christmas crackers by artist Brett McCormack bring understated drama to a holiday table. / A summer table in the open air by Charlotte Moss is a medley of lavender and lilac hues.

from left: Shades of warm orange, yellow, and gleaming brass are a sumptuous counterpoint to silver chargers and flatware. / A lunch setting by Kelli Ford in Dallas displays the fearless designer's trademark approach to pattern and color.

On the Upper East Side of Manhattan, Michael S. Smith uses a 19th-century marble table as the perfect platform for a disparate mix of materials—Spanish ceramics, copper mugs, intricately etched silver—with results that are nevertheless harmonious.

A table by Hutton Wilkinson is an ingenious combination of the colorful and refined, including antique vermeil cups and saucers, silver flatware, rock-crystal votives, and custom fabrics.

Quality

Cut-crystal candlesticks and hand-painted dinner plates edged in gold are just a few overt signs of quality that might make an impression at a dinner party. But quality isn't merely about price or provenance, it's also about buying smarter and better—when shopping for quality, less is often more. Eschew trends and stick with the classics. When it comes to your meal, these same dictates apply: Have a sense of where your food comes from. Is the chicken free-range, the fish ethically sourced, the fruits organic, and the vegetables non-GMO? Is the after-dinner coffee fair-trade? It can be dizzying, and a host should do the best he or she can without being stymied by trying to check all the boxes. And when it comes to quality tableware, the best of the best can be mixed in with vintage finds and heirloom pieces. In today's throwaway society, quality means more than ever before, and your guests will appreciate your efforts to provide an authentic experience.

right: A well-stocked bar includes options for every inclination. *below:* Top-drawer elements like custom Murano-glass goblets and antique Chinese porcelain mingle flawlessly. *opposite:* A breezy table composed of objects that have integrity is more than the sum of its parts.

Is it handcrafted? Homegrown? *Quality* is about celebrating authenticity and looking for the best, not necessarily the most expensive.

The boxwood garden at Keith Robinson's farm in Georgia is a serene backdrop for a stunning arrangement that stars David Austin roses.

R
Roses

Flowers were discussed earlier, but roses really deserve an entry of their own, don't they? The reasons are myriad, as are the colors and varieties, which make roses so dependable and adaptable for most any occasion. For any host, whether a novice or a master, roses are the most forgiving flower—they are readily available, completely reliable, and always, always a crowd-pleaser. Whether you choose a few superlong stems to place in one tall vase or a smattering of tightly clipped blooms displayed in low bowls scattered across a table, roses are the go-anywhere, do-anything flowers that never fail to impress. And for an impromptu, last-minute get-together with friends when a florist is out of reach, they are often the flower du jour at the local grocer. What could be better?

from left: Barely ripe berries on the branch capture the nuanced tones of orange blooms. / A symphony in pink pairs David Austin roses with Sarah Bernhardt peonies—and napkins to match.

from left: Antique and vintage Chinese porcelain sets the stage for a fireworks display of blossoms. / A low posy of roses with hydrangeas subtly echoes the pattern on 18th-century Russian porcelain.

RSVP

No matter one's age, there's still something thrilling about receiving an invitation: Hey, I'm going to a party! In today's world, electronic save-the-dates and e-vites are perfectly acceptable and can excite anticipation in your guests, but don't underestimate the significance of a printed invitation. In an increasingly virtual world, where few of us ever receive so much as a handwritten letter, the tactile sensation of opening an invitation can be the best beginning to your event. And who hasn't saved a beautiful invitation in a scrapbook or framed it as a reminder of a special occasion? Sadly, as our social graces have become more relaxed, people seemingly no longer RSVP with the same rigor as they once did. This discourtesy often leaves the host scrambling to accommodate a flurry of last-minute confirmations or cancellations, creating undue stress on the evening. So be the perfect guest, just as you would be the perfect host, and send along your RSVP immediately upon receipt (even if it's just for dinner around a friend's kitchen table)!

An open-plan scheme in the upstate New York house of Selina van der Geest lends a casual grace to a beguiling holiday table.

Seating Arrangements

Preparing for your perfect party requires a lot of planning (sometimes even plotting and scheming!), but at some point, the host has to let go. That's when magic and serendipity come into play. Orchestrating seating at a dinner requires the tact of a diplomat and a psychologist's understanding of human behavior. But don't be intimidated, and don't be afraid to mix people up—put the two people you think must be polar opposites next to each other. Seat your most talkative friend next to someone who seems shy. Polarizing individuals should be near someone who knows how to rein in the conversation if need be. And the dictum of boy-girl-boy-girl placement may seem old-fashioned, but there's also something endearing about it too, mainly because it works. Perhaps most importantly, remember that it's your table and your party. Sit by someone you like and love to talk to, because if everything else goes south, you'll still have a good chat.

right: Bunny Williams sets a lush table in the conservatory of her Connecticut residence, built from a salvaged greenhouse. *below:* Local flora decorates individual place settings at Colette van den Thillart's Canadian lake house. *opposite:* A formal setting in a New York apartment by Courtney Coleman and Bill Brockschmidt includes place cards and bread plates.

There is an *art and science* to creating a cohesive seating arrangement. It helps to have a little bit of luck on your side too.

left: A silver tray and cocktail accessories raise the stakes on game night. *below:* Hutton Wilkinson combines elaborate pieces with opulent fabrics. *opposite:* Tammy Connor mixes in heirloom pieces with everyday objects.

Silver

Silver, like good manners and gracious entertaining, endures. And despite its aristocratic connotations and associations with great wealth, silver is completely attainable. Whether it's a little or a lot, a saltbox or a samovar, silver adds a note of celebration to any event. With all apologies to *Downton Abbey*, it doesn't require a staff to maintain and care for silver. Nor should you be intimidated by the idea—just don't plan on setting your entire table in silver. Mix it up: If you're using your wedding silver, set it with the everyday china. If you are serving from the grand tureen you inherited from your grandmother, use porcelain for the other dishes. Silver, like gold, is one of those things that historically increases in value, but this should not be your raison d'être. Invest wisely and buy silver because you love it. Your joy in having something you love—and something you use regularly—will contribute to creating a comfortable and convivial table that welcomes your guests.

right: A 19th-century Italian wine cooler draws the eye in Susan Gutfreund's sitting room. *below:* In Michelle Nussbaumer's Swiss chalet, silver pitchers become part of the decor. *opposite:* In her Dallas home, Nussbaumer displays antique English pieces on a vintage cabinet.

Nothing beats the *glamour* that a singular piece of silver can add to a dining experience.

A Norwegian bowl and English tray give cherries and a selection of chocolate a grand sense of occasion.

From tall candlesticks and curvaceous pitchers to petite place card holders, beautiful, lustrous *silver* always has a spot at any well-adorned table.

A tray of bubbly circulates at Ann Getty's home in San Francisco.

Toasts

Some people excel at giving impromptu toasts, while others stammer and clam up completely. What the gracious host never wants to do is implore an unsuspecting or unwilling guest into making a toast. Like so many things in life, preparedness is the key, and if some poor soul is commanded to make remarks unaware, embarrassment could ensue. Similarly, the host herself should always be well prepared to make a toast. No matter one's level of confidence or assuredness in one's own abilities to perform extemporaneously, it is always wise to make a few notes ahead of time to keep your remarks sharp and focused. Speaking of focus, remember that the goal of the toast is to honor your guest, not to polish and put a shine on your own oratorical skills. When you toast, celebrate the beauty of brevity!

clockwise from top left: Premixing cocktails before guests arrive gives a host more time to mingle. / An option of red or white wine is sometimes all the selection you need. / A rustic wine cooler matches an outdoor California setting. / Champagne is the ultimate special-occasion standby. / Rosé on ice. *opposite:* Alessandra Branca offers port with biscotti for dessert.

In Istanbul, Antony Todd opts out of a tablecloth in favor of a linen runner that allows the grain of the table to show through and feels carefree.

Understated

Being understated must be the most understated value of all time—increasingly so today. In a culture where bigger is better and more, more, more typically wins the day, it can sometimes be—perhaps even unconsciously—tempting to go ever so gently over the top when one entertains. My advice: Don't. Nothing transmits confidence more than the ability to bring a sense of refined understatement to the tenor of your event. The tone is set by you and goes beyond the tangibles that your guest may experience: the food, the wine, the music, and the conversation. You are in control of all these elements and must leave little to chance. A potluck is fine, but that's not what this book is about. It is about how to define and refine the elements, many of which may seem intangible, that conspire to make an event magical. Understatement requires the ability to pull back and assess the tableau you are creating with a discerning and critical eye. Are the flowers too much? Is the table overladen with cutlery and china? Is the lighting perfect? The bottom line: Edit, edit, edit.

right: In Los Angeles, Windsor Smith ends a meal with dessert served family-style in the great room. *below:* Shawn Henderson's easeful setup in upstate New York includes a streamlined eat-in kitchen. *opposite:* An enormous oak tree on Brooke and Steve Giannetti's Ojai, California farm creates a shady spot for a divine open-air dining room.

Understated entertaining doesn't have to equate to being boring. A well-edited tablescape offers *breathing room* and a certain level of refinement.

A Beverly Hills estate by Daniel Cuevas adroitly incorporates plein air spaces into a coolly sophisticated indoor/outdoor scheme.

An otherwise humble arrangement of garden lilacs is suddenly bewitching in a beveled crystal vase.

Vases

Vases and vessels add that extra dimension that transmits a message to underscore the tone of the evening, whether it's casual or fancy, serious or fun. There is a difference between hosting a dinner for a visiting diplomat and the artist-in-residence at the university, and every detail you select creates the ineffable thing called "atmosphere" that helps people know what is and is not appropriate for tonight. No matter how formal your evening may be, though, it does not have to be so serious to the point of being somber. Similarly, no matter how casual the intention of your gathering, the accoutrements don't need to be informal. Indeed, why not turn expectations upside down? Instead of cut crystal and grand arrangements, soften the scale of your formal event: Consider stone planters or galvanized tins; choose a scattering of bud vases rather than a centerpiece; fill bowls with gorgeous vegetables to create a chic cornucopia. For that more casual affair, keep everything simple, but knock it out of the park with a grand arrangement approximating a Dutch still-life painting or a collection of exquisite glass vases holding nothing but your guest's imagination.

A stylish *vase* can be a fanciful addition to a glamorous setting or a grounding element in a sea of stuff.

Cindy, a Simmental cow from a neighboring farm, pops into Michelle Nussbaumer's Swiss escape. A handmade headdress adds a whimsical touch.

Welcoming

As the host, you have many duties, but my three cardinal rules for making guests feel truly welcomed are: Be punctual, be dressed, and don't exude stress. (I can't tell you the number of parties I've been to where the host is super tardy—there have even been a couple where the host has been in the shower or come down the hallway with wet hair wrapped in a towel.) Create conversation where there is none and don't get monopolized by one guest to the detriment of others. Exiting a conversation with someone monopolizing your time is tricky, but the host has a better excuse than anyone else—the chicken's in the oven! Offer to refresh their drink at the bar, even if it's full. If yours is still full, just say that you want to switch to something else and scoot away. If you've burned the main course, call for takeout. Your guests will understand; the worst thing you can do is share bad

right: A leafy arbor is an ideal spot for lunch on a Santa Barbara, California, estate by Ann Holden. *opposite:* Colette van den Thillart stages dinner at dusk on the dock of her Canadian lakeside cabin.

energy with them. A good host knows when to end the evening. Often, hosts think guests are having such a great time that they don't want to leave, but guests also don't want to be rude. I used to have a fear of being the first one to leave a dinner, but now I wear that badge proudly. As soon as I get up, a small cadre almost always follows me, and I swear I see a twinkle in the host's eye (or maybe it's exhaustion!).

In the gardens of a Saint-Tropez, France, villa designed by Piero Castellini Baldissera, ample outdoor tables accommodate a rotating cast of summer guests.

In his Highlands, North Carolina, cabin, John Oetgen deftly mixes moods and eras—gaucho chairs and an Indian tablecloth, a Bertoia sculpture and zebra-print rugs—into an ineffably stylish setting.

X Factor

How do you bring the X factor — by definition, an indescribable quality that makes something special — into action when planning your event? How do you make something intangible real? Memorable meals and special evenings often linger with us long after they are over for so many reasons. Was it a night on a grand terrace when the lighting, the sky, and the temperature conspired to create perfection? Or was it a candlelit, humble meal shared in someone's kitchen that made you feel warm and welcomed? Whatever it was, it's not always a good idea to replicate it exactly. As has been said earlier, entertaining involves a bit of magic and luck, and if an event exceeded your wildest expectations, don't feel defeated if you can't replicate it. You could serve the exact same meal on the same dishes in the same place the following week and have an entirely different take on it. Bask in the enjoyment of the memory, and make your next party even better than the one before.

A striking wallpaper on the ceiling of Michelle Nussbaumer's Dallas house electrifies a dining room in icy aqua hues.

A gift awaits under a framed collection of butterfly specimens in Tammy Connor's Alabama office.

You're Welcome

You are not only the consummate host of your own beautiful evenings, you are also the guest at many—hopefully equally beautiful—events at others' homes. How do you let the hostess know that you are delighted to be welcomed there? Selecting the appropriate hostess gift demonstrates not only your appreciation for the invitation, but also your own thoughtfulness and discernment. It is a tacit acknowledgement of mutual respect and, if chosen wisely, something that brings joy to the host. The lists of what not to bring are legion: nothing living (no goldfish!), no cut flowers that require the host to arrange them in a vase on the spot, and nothing perishable in general (you may love that 25-year-old Gouda, but not everyone does). And under no circumstances may you regift—you never know who is going to be at that party! Two exceptions to the prohibition against perishables are wine and chocolate. Again, not everyone loves these two things, but almost every host will keep them on hand for those who do. But if you bring these or any other comestibles as a hostess gift, don't expect it to be shared with everyone that night. A gift is a gift, not a summons to serve.

With the addition of clementines still on the branch, a pile of party favors has the romance of a still life.

215

Elda and Nicola Fabrizio eat most of their meals alfresco during the summer under the grape arbor of their villa in Lipari, an island off the coast of Sicily.

Zen

Zen is not a religion with a lot of rules; it is a state of mind and a way of being. Contrary to what many of us might assume, creating a Zen-like environment has little to do with decor, the choice of color, the scale and design of one's things, or the embrace of Asian aesthetics. Being Zen is being mindful of the moment by embracing your present surroundings and eliminating anxiety, distraction, and frustration. How you do this is up to you. Each of us knows what we are and are not good at doing. On a special night, don't present yourself with an unforeseen obstacle because you want to make the event memorable. Stick to your areas of competency. Making yourself comfortable is the first step to making your guests feel the same way. Perhaps the best way to do this is to take a page from the Zen playbook and practice a little meditation. Nothing sets the

right: A glass of Champagne offers a moment of respite in Charlotte Moss's East Hampton garden. *opposite:* A butler retreats down a hallway in Ann Getty's San Francisco residence.

night off on the wrong foot like a harried host, so plan. Make sure to build in time before welcoming your guests so that you can sit in a place of perfect calm for fifteen minutes or so before opening the door to your company. You'll be more content and peaceful, and your guests will be too. And long after those guests have left, the lights have been turned off, and the candles have been blown out, they'll recall your party—the best party of all. Cheers!

Photo credits

© **Melanie Acevedo:** 19, 21 (left), 24 (upper left), 28 (left), 43 (right), 55 (right), 76, 93 (left), 124, 134, 141 (right), 182 (left), 202, interior and landscape design by Michelle Nussbaummer, produced by Carolyn Englefield; 21 (right), 70, 112, 179, interior design by Bill Brockschmidt & Courtney Coleman, produced by Carolyn Englefield; 25, 46, 51 (left), 90 (left), 108 (left), 154, 173 (left), 188, 219, interior design by Ann Getty, produced by Carolyn Englefield; 30, 95 (right), 141 (left), 156, 173 (right), 182 (right), interior design by Susan Gutfreund, produced by Carolyn Englefield; 31 (right), 57 (left), 162 (right), 174 (left), 218, interior design by Charlotte Moss, architecture by Dale Booher, landscape design by Lisa Stamm, produced by Carolyn Englefield; 120 (right), 158, 164, 190 (upper right), produced by Catherine Lee Davis; 183, 210, Interior design by Michelle Nussbaummer, produced by Carolyn Englefield; 190 (lower right), Interior design by Windsor Smith, directed by Carolyn Englefield

courtesy of aidangrayhome.com: 200 (top middle)

courtesy of Alain Saint Joanis: 86 (7th row), 87 (4th row)

courtesy of Asprey: 105 (bottom 2nd from right)

Jesus Ayala/Studio D: 138 (bottom left)

courtesy of Baccarat: 104 (top 2nd and 3rd from left), 201 (middle)

© **Quentin Bacon:** 42 (left), 128 (middle), 190 (middle, upper left), interior design by Quinn Pofahl, architecture by Fred Smith, produced by Carolyn Englefield

@ **Sylvie Becquet:** 17, 66, 75, 77, 129, 136 (left), 152, 169, produced by Catherine Lee Davis

© **Alexandre Bilhache:** 206, interior and landscape design by Piero Castellini Baldessera, produced by Carolyne Englefield

courtesy of Bodo Sperlein: 87 (11th row)

courtesy of Buccellati: 186 (upper right)

courtesy of Cambridge Silversmith: 86 (9th row)

courtesy of Casafina: 53 (2nd row right)

courtesy of Christie's Images Ltd, 2016: 52 (2nd row left)

courtesy of Christofle: 187 (upper right)

Pamela Cook/Studio D: 86 (2nd row left, 4th row left, 8th row), 104 (bottom left), 138 (top left), 139 (top left), 187 (middle left)

Christopher Coppola/Studio D: 138 (middle right)

Courtesy of Croghan's Jewel Box: 186 (upper left)

© **Roger Davies:** 94 (left), 122, interior design by Christina Rottman, architecture by Bob Easton, landscape design by Douglas Hoerr, floral design by Laura Sangas, produced by Carolyn Englefield

courtesy of Devinecorp.net: 53 (bottom left)

Craig Dillon/courtesy of Wiener Silber Manufactur: 187 (middle right)

© **Erica George Dines:** 35, interior design by Susan Ferrier, architecture by Bobby McAlpine and Greg Tankersley; back cover (portrait)

courtesy of ebraunnewyork.com: 138 (top right)

courtesy of Eric Roinestad: 200 (top right)

© **Miguel Flores-Vianna:** 20 (left), 42 (right), 51 (right), 97 (right), interior design by Mary McDonald, architecture by Elmer Grey; 24 (middle), 144, 168 (right), 192

courtesy of Georg Jensen: 186 (bottom middle)

© **Tria Giovan:** 24 (upper right), 121 (left)

Alison Gootee/Studio D: 52 (upper right, 3rd row left), 53 (upper right), 86 (4th row left, 10th row left), 87 (1st row, 3rd row), 104 (bottom right), 200 (top left, bottom left, bottom right)

© **courtesy of Haviland:** 52 (2nd row right)

© **Aimee Herring:** 101, 184, recipes by Michele Chauvin Hieger, produced and styled by Mary Jane Ryburn

© **Thibault Jeanson:** 48 (left), 95 (left), 113 (lower left), 126, 163 (left), 174 (right), interior design by Charlotte Moss, floral design by Zeze, produced by Carolyn Englefield; 73 (right), 100 (upper right), 102, 119, 146 (upper left), 191, interior design by Alessandra Branca, produced by Carolyn Englefield, food styled by Lisa Sari Schoen

courtesy of John Stefanidis: 187 (upper center)

© **Max Kim-Bee:** 2, 57 (right), interior design by Tara Shaw, architecture by Barry Fox, landscape design by Byron Adams and Wanda Metz Chase, produced by Carolyn Englefield; 18, 56, 58, 60, 68 (left), 84, 97 (left), 110, 113 (middle), 128 (lower left), 163 (right), 166, 168 (left), 175, 178 (right), produced by Carolyn Englefield; 24 (lower right), 100 (lower right), 125, 216, interior design by Nicola and Elda Fabrizio, produced by Carolyn Englefield; 26, interior design by Peter Dunham, architecture by Andrew Franz Architect, produced by Carolyn Englefield; 31 (left), 49, 62, 64, 116, 146 (lower left), architecture and interior design by Robert Couturier, landscape design by Miranda Brooks, produced by Carolyn Englefield; 32, 73 (left), 128 (upper right), interior design by Stephen Sills, produced by Carolyn Englefield; 40, 44, 94 (right), 128 (lower right), interior and landscape design by Randy Korando and Dan Belman, produced by Carolyn Englefield and Leslie Newsom Rascoe; 55 (left), 72 (right), 80, 113 (upper left), 148, 162 (left), 176, Interior design by Selina Van Der Geest, produced by Carolyn Englefield; 82 (right), interior design by Amanda Nisbet, architecture by stuart L. Disston, landscape design by Bradford Kent Spaulding, produced by Carolyn Englefield; 83, architectural renovation and interior design by Bobby McAlpine, original architecture by Robert Anderson, produced by Caroyln Englefield; 91, 178 (left), 205, interior design by Colette Van Den Thillart, architecture by Wayne Swadron, landscape design by Black Rock Landscapes, produced by Carolyn Englefield; 96, interior design by Julie Hayes, renovation architecture by Larry E. Boerder Architects, landscape architecture by Paul Fields, produced by Mary Jane Ryburn, styled by Mary Jane Ryburn and Olga Naiman; 196, interior design by Daniel Cuevas, architecture by Kevin Clark, produced by Carolyn Englefield; 204, interior design by Ann Holden, architecture by Warner Group Architects, produced by Carolyn Englefield; 208, interior design and architecture by John Oetgen, produced by Carolyn Englefield

© **Francesco Lagnese:** 20 (right), 22, 113, 146 (upper right, middle), 194 (left), interior design by Shawn Henderson, produced by Carolyn Englefield; 48, 109,160 (right), 180 (left), 198, produced by Eugenia Santiesteban Soto and Carolyn Englefield; 50, 130, 132, 172 (left), 180 (right), 190 (lower left), interior design by Hutton Wilkinson, produced by Carolyn Englefield; 68 (right), 77 (right), 108 (right), 114, 140 (left), 181, 212, 214, interior design by Tammy Connor; 175, interior design by Celerie Kemble, architecture by Lichten Craig Architecture + Interiors, produced by Carolyn Englefield

Erika LaPresto/Studio D: 52 (third row center); 138 (bottom right), 139 (bottom right), 186 (bottom right and left), 187 (bottom left), 201 (top, bottom left)

Charlotte Jenks Lewis/Studio D: 86 (11th row), 139 (bottom left)

© **Thomas Loof:** 59, 89, 92, 93 (right), 100 (middle) 136 (right), 140 (right), 170, 172 (right)

© **David Meredith:** 28 (right), 150 © **James Merrell:** 69, 72 (left), 100 (lower left), 137, interior design by Elizabeth Locke, produced by David M. Murphy

Marko Metzinger/Studio D: 87 (7th row, 9th row), 105 (bottom right)

courtesy of Michael Aram: 86 (2nd row left)

courtesy of Michael Verheyden: 200 (center row left)

courtesy of Moser USA: 105 (middle)

J Muckle/Studio D: 86 (1st row left, 6th row, 10th row right)

© **David Oliver:** 43 (left), interior design by Veere Grenney Associates, produced by Carolyn Englefield

courtesy of Paravicini.it: 52 (bottom right, bottom left, 3rd row right), 53 (2nd row left)

courtesy of Pia Wustenberg: 200 (center)

Susan Pittard/Studio D: 104 (2nd row left), 105 (bottom 2nd from left)

Courtesy of Puiforcat: 187 (bottom right)

courtesy of Richard Ginori: 52 (upper left)

Lara Robby/Studio D: 86 (3rd row, 5th row left), 87 (10th row, 6th row), 104 (top right), 105 (left x3), 138 (center left), 201 (bottom middle)

Emily Kate Roemer/Studio D: 52 (bottom middle)

© **Lisa Romerein:** 37 (left); 195, interior design by Steve and Brooke Giannetti, architecture by Steve Giannetti, landscape design by Steve Giannetti and Margaret Grace, Grace Design Associates, written by Frances Schultz

courtesy of Saint-Louis: 104 (left second from bottom)

© **Annie Schlechter:** 50 (right), 100 (upper left), 106, 113 (lower right), interior design by Richard Keith Langham, produced by Carolyn Englefield; 98,interior design by Jane Hawkins Hoke, architecture by James Carter, landscape design by Norman Kent Johnson, produced by David M. Murphy

Studio D: 104 (2nd row left)

courtesy of Tom Dixon: 201 (bottom right)

© **Luca Trovato:** 24 (lower left), 29, 38, 82 (right), 146 (lower right), 194 (right), interior design by Windsor Smith, directed by Carolyn Englefield, styled by Jody Kennedy, food styled by Rori Trovato

David Turner/Studio D: 86 (5th row right), 139 (top right)

Stuart Tyson/Studio D: 53 (bottom right), 87 (2nd row), 105 (top center, 138 (center), 200 (bottom right)

© **Mikkel Vang:** 8, 10, 11, 12, 13, 23 (right), 37 (right), interior design by Kathryn M. Ireland, produced by Carolyn Englefield

courtesy of Varga Art Crystal: 104 (bottom second from right)

courtesy of Venini: 201 (center row left)

courtesy of Vietri: 87 (8th row)

© **Bjorn Wallander:** cover, 6, 36, 78, interior design by Kate Cordsen, landscape design by River-End Lanscaping, produced by Carolyn Englefield & Anne Foxley; 14, 23, 90, 120, 142, produced by Carolyn Englefield; 54, 128, 147, 160, 161, interior design by Daniel Romualdez, produced by Carolyn Englefield; 121, interior design by Suzanne Kasler, architecture by Madison Spencer, landscape design by Riley & Associates, produced by Robert Rufino

courtesy of Wedgewood: 53 (upper left)

courtesy of William Yeoward Crystal: 104 (bottom second from left), 105 (top right), 187 (upper left)

Index

Note: Page references in **bold** indicate primary discussions. Page references to photos indicate caption locations.

HEARSTBOOKS

An Imprint of Sterling Publishing Co., Inc.
1166 Avenue of the Americas
New York, NY 10036

VERANDA is a registered trademark of Hearst Communications, Inc.

ISBN 978-1-61837-222-2

Distributed in Canada by Sterling Publishing Co., Inc.
c/o Canadian Manda Group, 664 Annette Street
Toronto, Ontario, Canada M6S 2C8
Distributed in the United Kingdom by GMC Distribution Services
Castle Place, 166 High Street, Lewes, East Sussex, England BN7 1XU
Distributed in Australia by NewSouth Books
45 Beach Street, Coogee, NSW 2034, Australia

For information about custom editions, special sales, and premium and corporate purchases,
please contact Sterling Special Sales at 800-805-5489 or specialsales@sterlingpublishing.com.

Manufactured in China

2 4 6 8 10 9 7 5 3 1

www.sterlingpublishing.com

Design by Suzanne Noli